Little Grey Bird

Poetic Recollections

by

Caroline Brae

Acknowledgements

I want to express gratitude to my husband, Chris, for his support, encouragement, and technical assistance in the creation of *Little Grey Bird*.

A special thank you to the National Media Services, Inc., team, especially Mary Carnahan, whose finesse and attention to detail helped to bring my vision to life.

Editor: Linda J. Kobert

Cover Art and Design: Caroline Brae

Printed in the USA by National Media Services

Inquiries and Mail Orders:

Contact poet at Caroline.Brae@gmail.com

Little Grey Bird

Contents

For my Dad

Who taught me how to fly

Grey Haze

A quiet departure
After a valiant fight
On the 20th
Half past midnight

Suddenly the hours
Seemed to stand still
Blackness turned to dawn
And thin air chilled

My heart breaking open
My hand holding yours
I knew that your life
Would be no more

I walked into darkness
A clear, bright night
One star was added
When your soul took flight

Picture of You

There is a picture of you
Quietly stored within
My little pink flip phone
Sitting in my dresser drawer
One of many places my heart resides

I wear your gold wedding ring
Secured on my finger
By my antique silver band
It keeps you close to me
It keeps me close to you

I took a picture of you
The day you turned 80 years old
Cleaned up in a white shirt
With navy blue pants
To go see the doctor

The final prognosis
Cancer—Terminal—Stage IV
One to six months he said
You passed within 30 days
Fading before my eyes

Still you remained as always
Full of love, dignity, and grace
You loved until the very end
This time your hand in mine
You playfully asking, "Who do I have here?"

Every day I greet with a smile
My favorite older photograph
Both of us happy and healthy
Holding our brimmed hats
In our hands—daughter like father

Every day I still say
"Hello Dad - Good morning"
And I can still hear your reply
"Hel-lo Car-o-line." Your voice
Rippling my name like a songbird

Reduced to Zero

It was my breaking point
The day I felt how 9/11 looked
Long after the towers fell
An act of personal terrorism
A dark grey choking haze
Suffocating my last hope
One big hellhole in my heart
My head well below sea level
Ground zero—the day I fell
Like the tall pillars of NYC
I came tumbling down
Nothing left when the smoked cleared
Nothing
Zero

Stolen Splendor

Splendid, resplendent
No, it is not true
Shrouded, suffocating
Underneath an invisible
Menacing cloud
That steals happiness
Sucking life out of you
Splendid, resplendent
An unfulfilled wish
Lost, scattered
Smashed by the wind
Leaving me broken hearted
Leaving me broken
Leaving me
Alone

I am the Other

This, that, and the other
"Whatnots," she said
"Want not," said another
I was always the other
At best, considered quirky
At worst, the black sheep
Or pitied as the barren one
Or dismissed with a laugh
From the ones who said,
"All he has to do is look at me
And I get pregnant"
All the doctors, all the prayers
All the tears in the world
Could not ease the pain
Of whatnot, want not
Whatever...
I am the other

Ponderings

"Go," he said, "Find your process"
Whatever does that mean?
Process—Like food for thought?
Ideas that simmer until boiled
So thoroughly pondered over and over
Until there is no place left to go but out
Out of my head, out of my mind
Out of my heart, from me to you
"Be honest," he instructed
"They will know if you are skirting issues"
Issues—those personal obstacles
That get in the way of letting go
Go and be honest
Find your process
Let go
Fly

Suspended

Small ordinary details fill my room
A discarded dresser, an old lamp,
And a faded photograph
Reflect back in a mirror
Hanging from my door distorting
Otherwise unremarkable items
My soft white feathery bedding
Floats like a cloud high above
Chaos and chatter below
And I rest among skyscrapers
Waiting anxiously to find my place
Where countless others have flocked
To search out a new life
One that is neither full nor empty
Simply filled with promise
Of what may come tomorrow

Although hidden from my view
The Empire State Building
Shines a silver reflection
Upon my bed and points
Not upwards or downwards
But simply away
Out into the ever-changing sky
And the skyline of a constantly
Moving city, the apple of my eye
First brought me here
To this place of dreams
Where clatter becomes music
And shadows learn to dance
Where words flash across
Neon billboards and night
Does not sleep

It is the daylight that warms
My spirit, regardless if
Life is turned upside down
And I cannot tell north from south
Only east and west
A reflection of the unseen icon
Illuminates my path with a silver dusting
And continues to point me
Out and away from the warped images
Of a limited life tucked behind a closed door
Where all my fears reside
Standing at the corner of W34th and 5th Avenue
I choose to trust the silver cables
And rise as high as steel beams
And thin air can take me
To find my true north

Inspired by Abelardo Morell, Camera Obscura:
The Empire State Building (1994)

Resurgence

You cook, but don't eat
Starving yourself of the warmth
Provided by hot, nurturing food
Prepared by loving hands
That serve others, God, and country
Hands that cared long and hard
For those beaten down in the path
Searching for justice where there is none
Fighting to protect others from the unseen
Trying to make this place we call home
A better, safer place
For your children, for others
For the future, for now
Wars seem to last longer
An endless fight with no clear
Dividing line of safe borders
The enemy, a constant moving target
In unknown lands in hidden places
Until they strike unexpectedly
The innocent ones, the ones unprotected
No armor or arms to rise up
To stop the violence or hatred
Those of one God detest any other
Not recognizing we are all God's children
Put on this earth to do good deeds
Not to harm others, or this earth
War does not bring peace
It does not cleanse our hearts
Or minds—Destruction lingers
Long after the damage is done
If only you could
See yourself as I do
Slowly roasting warmth and flavor
Back into your life

Convergence

Intrigued by my voiceless image
A face barely seen beneath
Sunglasses, lime green floppy hat,
And plaid wool scarf
A temporary glimpse
Of the woman behind the lens
Or hidden in the shadowy reflections
Of a chapel window honoring
Fallen soldiers from an uncivil war
It isn't a game we play
It is an exchange in an electronic world
Where photos are shared in instant squares
With captions sometimes short
Other times long, with the resulting
Longing of places and people
Ones you can sense, but cannot touch
Nights are long and
Mornings come early
Conversing with a friend
Across invisible lines
Where there are no words
Or explanations for feelings
For those unseen, illuminating
Beings of light whose frames
Create a sense of connection
In the silence of midair

Metamorphic Urgency

The morning starts slowly
As the light gains strength
To shine upon a new day
Full of possibilities
To change or remain unaltered
Stay or go, I realize
Deep inside I am
The same, regardless
If I am here or there
Motionless or moving
Frantically in many directions
My core is my rock
A foundation upon
Which to build

My true nature
Is alive and will be well
If I tend to it
Like a rock, I
Weather the storms
Soaked and sometimes
Shattered by harsh winds
Or greedy hands
Pounding at my soul
Yet somehow I survive
To see another day
And decide if I
Shall stay or go
In the end, I am
Alone with myself
Until I decide if
My heart has wings
Even though my feet
Are firmly planted
In shifting soil

I find the stillness
In my running
My eternal fight
Against damning demons
I take flight
And head towards
The light
With a rock
In my pocket

Tucked

Yours, Mine, and Ours
I do, you do, until...
Broken promises, broken dreams
Hurt hearts, then tempers flare
Unkind words in harsh tones
Create angry spirits
And make it difficult to sleep
Yet somehow you convince me
Comfort is to be found
Tucked beneath your arm
Resting gently on your shoulder
Sleep comes unexpectedly
On your side of the bed
Yours, Mine, and Ours

Morning Dance

Delicate whispers
Gently floating down
From sky to earth
Taking a moment
To stop and dance
Temporarily swirling
In undetermined directions
Before touching softly
To the ground
Each one unique
Each one separate
Yet together they
Weave a blanket
Of pure delight
Somehow the world
Looks different
Covered in magic crystals
Misty haze surrounding
All that we know
Allowing us to see
A different view
A different light
A different life
Yes, things do indeed
Look different
In the snow

Passing By

Shoulder-length blonde hair
A passing view of a woman
Driving down a curvy country lane
Behind the wheel of a white SUV
Vehicle of choice for so many Americans
An illusion of safety after 9/11
A coating of protective armor
To cart children to soccer practice,
Dance class, or weekend gatherings
Thousands of pounds of steel
Maneuvered with a single hand
As she drinks from an adult sippy cup
A container with lid, and a long straw
Filled with a fountain beverage
Sugary sweetness with a punch of caffeine
To help her through her day
Perhaps sooth her weariness
From the hectic schedule of activities
That constitute her daily routine
I wonder if her dreams of marriage
Of children, perhaps a beautiful home,
And a prosperous life have been
Reduced to an empty car
Where she drives down the road alone
With her sippy cup in hand
I take a sip of water from my recycled bottle
And carefully check both lanes
Before putting my little five speed in gear
And heading on to yoga class
Wondering why I did not end up
With a sippy cup in my hand

Corner Spot

My corner spot remained open
Despite the fact I was running late
Thankfully, so was my instructor
A rare, if ever, occurrence
I placed my mat quickly, but neatly
And gathered a blanket, and bolster
Items I know she will use
To help us open our bodies
Which tighten up and close each day
From pushing too hard
From ongoing neglect
And not taking time
To slow down and stop

In order to benefit fully
You must settle into the silence
Of simply being still
The power of doing nothing
Will allow you to rise and expand
Find strength in balancing
Not only your body
But your mind and spirit
Thankful for my little corner
Feeling safely tucked away
I release my worldly cares
Landing quietly on my mat
I stay in silence
Awaiting the calm guidance
That is within
That is without
That simply is

Of Another Time and Place

She sneered and said,
"You don't belong here"
Her sour face spoke volumes
Of her unyielding attitude
Like so many Americans
She forgets we are all immigrants
From one time or another
She thinks I don't understand
The culture or values
Of an isolated mountain holler
But I know it

I know it like the back
Of my grandmother's hand
I know it from fire and brimstone
Of old time religion
That traveled with my family
As they attempted to escape
Absolute poverty,
Overwhelming desperation,
The Great Depression
My grandfather walked
From town to town
In search of work
To provide for his family
His search ultimately landed
Them all in a valley
Farther north
Where a factory
Provided steady, grinding
Shift work that made a man
Older than his years

She thinks I don't understand
Hardships, exclusion, torments
For my language, my uncanny notions
Taken from folklore long ago
Stories travel with people
Their true heritage tucked
Deep inside their souls
Despite outward appearances
Or corrected speech that
Sometimes fails and lends
A glimpse into another time
Another place you don't see

She only sees that my family
Left this place
What she does not see
Is what remains of the
Mountain culture
That pushed us all
To do better, be better
To step outside ourselves
To help others
To help anyone searching
For a better life
She might think
That I don't belong here
But the mountains are
My home
And they call out
My name ever so softly
And I listen closely
As I turn away from her sneer

Cabin by the Road

Drivin' down to Batesville
To a cabin by the road
Will I hear my voice a'callin'?
Will my stories go untold?
Will my demons come to fetch me?
Will I set my spirit free?
On the road down to Batesville
I wonder who I'll see

Tattered boards upon the front porch
See my shattered, lonely soul
As I walk up to the door step
I fear I should go home
There are skeletons in the closet
That have hid a long, long time
Do I keep the door closed tightly?
I don't know what I'll find

As the beams rise up to greet me
I feel weak but carry on
Will their strength come out to save me?
Inside this Batesville home
Solid beams of honey lumber
Woven tight and standin' strong
Will they give us each our courage?
To stand and sing our songs?

In this cabin down in Batesville
You can hear pure voices soar
And the wooden beams support you
As your fear stands at the door
Gentle eyes rise up to greet you
As your life comes floodin' in
In this cabin down in Batesville
The stories never end

Standing Ground

I stare at the wide planks beneath my feet
One-hundred-year-old Douglas fir
That grace my new abode in shades
Of burnt orange and black iron
Transforming it from cold to cozy

Thankfully, I stumbled upon them
In the scrap pile at the bottom
Of an old warehouse-turned-sawmill
I am a good bargain hunter
A skill I learned from my Dad

I searched until I found
The perfect foundation
For rebuilding my life
Carving out a space
In the place I call home

These warm sturdy floors
Serve as an anchor for me
A source of strength
To help me reclaim
My standing ground

Fire Water

Like fire upon fire
My passion raged
Not only for lost loves
But for a lost vocation
A lifetime of efforts,
Hopes, and dreams
For others outside myself
For others inside my world
Fire upon fire
Will destroy you
Consume you (it is said)
Leaving nothing
But ashes

Burning like a Phoenix
I rise, and rise again
Learning to quench my thirst
Put out the silent fires
That blaze in my soul
Until a libation
Sparks a flame
And I roar
Like a tin whistle
Then I remember
How and why
I landed here
Fire upon fire
Consumed me
And now I rise
From my ashes
Soaked in the morning rain

Cosmic Connection

Bursting forth
Like spring petals
Of a blossoming flower
Every fiber of my being
Exploding in ripples
Releasing stagnant energy
Forgotten feelings
Repressed emotions
Expressions long forgotten
But not lost

Somewhere beneath layers
Of should have's
Emerges a cosmic door
Opening to a universe
Previously unseen
Blocked by a black hole
Surrounded by dark matter
One ray of light
Streaming forth
Allowing access
To a night sky
Full of possibilities
Glimmering specs of hope
Dancing freely
Reaching tiny particles
That ultimately converge
Into a cosmic connection
Where everything
Is new again

I Am

I am my father's daughter
I am the quiet observer
Who sees slight nuance
And hears the incessant clatter
Of the loud, boisterous, and ego-centric
Family, friends, and passersby
I am the one sitting silently, often times
Not uttering a word
Yet whose unspoken voice speaks volumes
And whose thoughtful messages are received
Only by attending ever so closely
Redefining what it means to be strong
A silent protector with the warning of
One short phrase "Now listen here"
One who deflected animosity, anger, and hatred
Directed by loved ones or belligerent strangers
Through slow, deliberate, and concise
Movements and speech
Ever watchful, ever mindful
Of any hidden agendas or insincerity
Blessed with a working man's dignity
And a grace that cannot be taught
Only learned through hardships
And loving deeply, unselfishly

I am grateful for the lessons
My father imparted to me
His unassuming intelligence
One that surpassed university knowledge
A broadness of mind, an uncanny understanding
And wisdom that expanded my self-examination
My father is the one who told me to release
Years of harsh, bitter treatment
In three small words
"Let it go, Caroline"
And when it came time
To tell him goodbye
I echoed his words by saying
"You have loved us long enough.
You can let go now Dad."
I am my father's daughter
He taught me how to love
He taught me how to live
He taught me how to fly
In his final goodbye

About the Poet

Caroline Brae lives in the mountains of Central Virginia. A high school teacher of twenty-five years, she embraced the challenges of students with emotional and learning disabilities. Their struggles made her stronger and wiser. Caroline has since ventured on a ten-year creative and artistic odyssey dabbling in the performing arts as a choreographer, dancer, singer/songwriter, and pianist. *Little Grey Bird* is her first poetic endeavor in a long journey to find her voice.

Printed in the USA

ISBN 978 – 0 – 9978300 – 5 – 7 First Edition